MW01296110

WHEN I LEFT MY DADDY'S HOUSE

Publishing Consultant
The Pierce Agency, LLC, USA
www.ThePierceAgencyLLC.com
804.549.2884

Photo Courtesy of Nancy Jo Photography
Cover Design Courtesy of Sassi Creative, Inc.

Printed in the U.S.A.

For reprint permission, or to use text or graphics from this publication, e-mail your request to firstladymcknight@yahoo.com. To book Apostle Shirley Johnson for a speaking engagement, please send an email to danettamcknight@apostleshirleyjohnson.com.

TABLE OF CONTENTS

PREFACE

Ecclesiastes 3:1-8 reads:

1 To everything *there is* a season, and a time to every purpose un-

der the heaven:

2 A time to be born, and a time to die; a time to plant, and a time

to pluck up *that which is* planted;

3 A time to kill, and a time to heal; a time to break down, and a

time to build up;

4 A time to weep, and a time to laugh; a time to mourn, and a

time to dance;

5 A time to cast away stones, and a time to gather stones to-

gether; a time to embrace, and a time to refrain from embracing;

6 A time to get, and a time to lose; a time to keep, and a time to

cast away;

7 A time to rend, and a time to sew; a time to keep silence, and

a time to speak;

8 A time to love, and a time to hate; a time of war, and a time of

peace.

Everyone, if thought about, has experienced over half of

the verbs listed here and before life is over, will have experi-

enced them all. The key the lightbulb moment for you is the one in which you are in now. Are you aware of it? Will you obey and do what needs to be done in the proper time? I realized it was time for me to share the wondrous works of God in my life after 15 years of waiting. I gladly wish to let everyone know what motivates me to praise and worship God the way I do, and I pray and hope that it will inspire others to try and trust Him as well.

DEDICATION

To the Lord and savior of my life, Jesus Christ, the lover of my soul. To my children who are a major part of these writings: Bishop Semaj, Danetta, Anthony, Thomosa, Natasha, Derrick, Dominic, Stephanie and Jareth. To my very special grandchildren: Jalen, Semaja, Henre', Josiah and Jaden. And to my never to be forgotten parents, John and Mary Etta Nowell.

ACKNOWLEDGEMENTS

To the people of God that welcome the truth, for they will know the truth and it will set them free. To all the people of God that encouraged me to share my story for the sole purpose of being a blessing to someone else, and to give hope that it is not over until God says it is over. To my children who were the blessings that came from my afflictions, and who remembered and are along with me today, arise with praise and victory.

To Mr. Marquis Jelks who gave me that final push I needed after 15 years to finish and share my story so that others will know that there is hope!

When I Left My Daddy's House
By Shirley Johnson

INTRODUCTION

October 6, 1951, Jubilee Hospital in Henderson, North Carolina at 7 p.m. is a date, place and time that will never be forgotten by me. That, of course, is the date, place and time I was born! I don't remember ever having a birthday party, but Ma never forgot my birthday. She would start the day before reminding us of our birthdays and would then cook a delicious dinner. That was all I wanted and needed. My mother often told me that as a baby, I was small and had more hair than face. I was the ninth child, but my parents had a way of making you feel like an only child. Every child was unique and special to them; according to them, we were all going to go far in life, and whatever Ma and Daddy said was gospel to me.

My world consisted of my home and whatever small community we lived in, such as Henderson, Williamsboro or Townsville, just to name a few. These were small, adjoining communities where everybody knew everybody. And let's not forget going to church every Sunday! That was ok with me. I was happy.

The highlight of any given day was when Daddy took a couple of us kids with him to the grocery/dry goods/service station store and he got whatever was needed for the house and then allowed us to get a couple pieces of bubblegum - blow gum, as he would call it. The man behind the counter would give it to me in my very own little brown bag! I never understood why Daddy oftentimes did not pull out his money but would sign a piece of paper handed to him by the man behind the counter. Boy, did my Daddy have it going on! He got whatever he wanted and didn't have to pay. Of course, I did not know that the owners knew him well enough to extend him credit, and later on, he would have to pay – and probably with a few more dollars added to it.

John Nowell was a phenomenal provider for all of those 13 children (losing one as an infant) and a wife, and he did it with perfection. I never remember a hungry day or a lack of proper clothing. Our homes were never dilapidated or unclean. Ma and Daddy were such good providers, I never knew we were considered poor.

Breakfast, dinner and supper consisted of everyone sitting at the table together having prayer, not a short one, but a long one; then, you could eat orderly. Oh! And you could eat as much as you could hold, but you could not waste any food because according to Ma, it was a sin. And as Ma said, any sin could get in the way of your Holy and Sanctified life with God. Even as children, we were taught about living a righteous life. Yes, we were Holy Rollers, and everyone in all the little adjoining towns knew we went to that "Holy' church in Townsville, NC.

Mount Calvary Holy Church was its name. It was a great event every Sunday, starting at home first around the kitchen table; the scripture first and then the prayer, which prepared us for church. I knew from the time we stepped in the door of the church until we left that it was going to be on: the music, the shouting (dancing), the screaming, the praying, and the testifying. Yes, this was my world, and it felt safe and secure.

The days and years passing by was something I did not worry about because Ma and Daddy were always going to be there. There was never a thought of them even getting old and perhaps dying one day because in my mind, they were always going to be there.

Everyone in the towns knew each other and shared what they had; they looked out for each other and each other's children. There was never a thought in my young mind that there was a totally different world and people out there, and that I would one day walk into it and get a rude, life-changing awakening.

In 1961, at the age of 10, my parents informed us of a major decision they had made; we were going to move. *Ok, move? Nothing so unusual or major about that,* I thought. I was used to moving. Where to this time?

We were already in Williamsboro, so Townsville? Henderson? No, not this time. Totally all together outside of North Carolina. Let me guess. Virginia? Yes! We were moving to Charlottesville, Virginia. How did I know? Because four of my older siblings had already moved there. They came home on holidays and would tell my father about the job opportunities and houses with toilettes inside, and of telephones and buses that carried you from one place to another for only a quarter, taxi cabs, and grocery stores that were separate from the gas stations, and best of all, not a town, but an actual city! It had all of the amenities we did not have.

Was I supposed to eavesdrop on grown folks' business? Nope, but I did anyway. I was curious that way. Daddy was a smart man, one who could only read the *Bible*, but made up for his illiteracy in every other kind of way. He put a lot of thought into moving, I'm sure; that's the way he was. He never rushed into anything. So, after much thought and consideration, we were on our way to Charlottesville, Virginia.

Oh, boy! Ten years old and I had never been out of the state of North Carolina. I was on the way to another state, a new school and new friends, a new house and most importantly, a new church! Was I scared? No, surprisingly I was not; as long as my security blankets, Ma and Daddy, were there, I was OK. What a difference to what I was used to; houses were close together, side by side on a street as opposed to houses being a ½ mile from each other and on secondary roads. *I could get used to this!*

There were a lot of things we left behind that even though we were not physically there, but memory-wise never, we would always be that family that feared God and still had prayer at the kitchen table. Personally, I will always remember the smell of the tobacco at the barnyard where my parents and older siblings oftentimes worked; surprisingly, it paid well, too. I will also never forget the sticky substance that came from the cucumbers when we picked them from the vines, and the panic attacks I would have that seemed to come out of nowhere; I'd run to my mother screaming, "I'm dying?" Where did they come from, we wondered? At the time, we did not have an answer, but now I do know. The HAND of God was upon me.

We were now out of Townsville, Williamsboro and Henderson, but the towns would always be in us and I'd always have my beautiful memories. The time I once thought was standing still, wasn't anymore. A fast-moving town dictated time moving faster, or so it seemed. My Daddy secured a job at the biggest hospital not only in Charlottesville, but in the whole wide world to me! You go, Dad! He went from being a miner and sharecropper to an employee in the housekeeping department at the University of Virginia Hospital, and I might add that his inability to read did not hinder him. Hallelujah! God was working on me, too, watching everything as it unfolded for us, and it was a good feeling.

John William Nowell moved on to do something he had never done before and that was to buy a house: 204 12th Street

S.W., or better known as "Gospel Hill." I never knew how the area had acquired its name, but it did not really even matter to me. We had our own house; we would never have to move again! EVER! My mom was hanging right in there, too. She supported John in whatever he endeavored to do; she knew him like that and to her, if John attempted something, it was going to work out. In the meantime, I was headed to Jefferson Elementary School: new teachers, a new system and new friends. Would I adjust? Did I want to adjust? Yes, I did and yes, I *did*.

By now, I was 12 years old and there was no big yellow school bus coming to take us to school; we had to walk in the winter, spring, summer and fall. No worries. It was not far from our home and I had discovered my own shortcut: down the railroad tracks, past the train station and onto Main Street, and down the street to Downey Street to the school door. Yes, I had it down to a science and was never late. So, things were good. My Dad had a job, brought a house, and we were enrolled in school. What was next was finding a church. But did I miss anything from Carolina? Was I homesick at all for anything back home? Shamefully, no! Everything was bigger and better, and might I add, more modern as well. Now this was the way people were supposed to live!

Although things were a lot better in Charlottesville, a lot of our African American neighbors lived in poverty. We now had indoor plumbing, plenty of sleeping space, and a nice size kitchen, which my mother was happy about. Some of our neighbors didn't have those needed things in their homes. Some of them still didn't have indoor plumbing or more bedroom space to accommodate their families. Which made me think my family was well. Even with that thought, my parents were always willing, and did share what we had with our neighbors. Daddy was still working, and Ma kept the house together and cooked those good meals every day. What was fast food? I didn't know and didn't care as long as I could get my hands on one of those biscuits, a piece of fried chicken, mashed potatoes and cabbage. Even though the kitchen was in the back of the house, you could smell the food when you stepped in the front door.

Our house was a big one: a two-story with four bedrooms, two kitchens, one bath. It did not matter that we had one bath because it was inside, and not outside. There were two other small rooms that were turned into bedrooms for cousins from Carolina who decided to join us; it was ok with Ma and Daddy. We had "arrived" and they were always reaching back to give somebody else a hand; that's where I got that attribute from and it plays a great part in who I am now! When you don't forget God, and don't forget others, there is no limit to your blessing. We are our brother's keeper and the more you give, the more God gives back to you. That's what we Nowells were taught and it worked, and still is working for me to this very day. O, Bless Him!

I was now 15 years old and in high school at Jackson P. Burley High School, an all-black school noted for one of the baddest bands in the state. I might also add that the schools in 1966 had not been integrated yet, but little did I know this was about to change. April 1966, one month and a half before school was to close, we had an assembly informing us that at the high school level – the first in Charlottesville - we had a choice to transfer to another high school – all-white – by the name of Lane High School to help start the integration or stay at Burley. But ultimately, in the future, we would not have a choice. We would have to accept the transfer.

Shirley Ann Nowell decided to take the transfer and went on to Lane High School, and until graduation. I decided to take the transfer because until this time in my young life, I had not socially interacted with any other race. No more than while in North Carolina, seeing the older white man that worked behind the counter at the corner store. Or the white gentleman that my father share cropped with, or paid rent to. But I never noticed any white children around. So again, I felt this decision was unexplainably something I had to do. I wanted to know if white people thought as I did. Would they accept and interact with me? I wanted to see if they were smarter than me. I had to find out, and I did.

My very first friend, after integrating to the high school, was a very helpful, polite, and nice young girl. She helped me find my classes after every period in a timely manner. She didn't seem to allow color to be a barrier between us. I found many others that made me feel the same way. They didn't make me feel intimidated or inferior to them, but they welcomed me and made me feel like a part of the school. Don't get me wrong! There were instances of alleged inequalities and prejudices, but

I was thankful that it didn't happen to me nor that I was a part of the treatment. And that was a wise decision on my part.

The time flew by fast as well. It is now June 1969, and I am graduating. I had big plans for my life, and it did not consist of marriage or children. I point these out because some of my girlfriends and classmates did not wait until graduating but were happily in the "family way" at 17 and 18. I was not mad at them. I had bigger plans for my life. I enrolled in Jefferson Professional Institute; an institute of business was my choice until I decided what I wanted to do permanently. While attending the institute, I was approached by a colleague about an upcoming Teaching Assistant (TA) position in a brand-new school opening in the city. She thought I would be the right one for it; it sounded good to me. I jumped right on it and was immediately hired. Jackson-Via was a moneymaker for the moment, and I was happy. Assisting the teachers and ultimately teaching by myself was my niche in life and little did I know was the beginning   of   my   ultimate   assignment.

Not only was my family now good and settled in Virginia but were very happy as well. All of us were employed and we had found a new church as well. The only way to describe the church is that it was a foot-stomping, handclapping, Pentecostal, tongue-talking church of the living God. When you got out of your car in the parking lot, you could feel the vibration of the praise going forth and it forced you to not waste a moment outside but to run in as fast as you could before the praises stopped! The prophetic word would go forth every service - the God said, and the Holy Ghost said - and truthfully, eight out of 10 were correct in what God and the Holy Ghost had said.

The Prophetic movement was new and overwhelming to some, but to me, I had experienced it throughout the years of my own life through my Daddy, a prophet in his own rite, as well as myself. I just didn't have the revelation as to the name of what it truly was.

It is now 1970 and our church membership was growing with such as those as should be saved, and along with the "such as s-h-o-u-l-d be saved," was a young man by the name of Earnest Wendell Carr. He was already familiar to my family because two of my family members were already married to two of his family members. So, he moved to the Charlottesville with his sister who was married to my brother. As some, but not all, of the young people often did, they made each other feel welcomed and helped them integrate with the other young people in the area.

I have always been a very easy person to get along with and often overextend a welcome, but at the same time, the prophetic discernment has always been in my life since I was a small girl. As time went on, I realized that Earnest's integration into the church was minimum at best; it was more focused on me. No problem! I knew what I was ready for and what I was not!!

I must acknowledge the personality of Earnest; he was soft-spoken, funny, friendly, spoiled, selfish, very irresponsible and, at times, he could be controlling. My family liked what they knew of him very much. Mr. Carr used all of the above traits to hone in on his target and that target was me. According to him, after the fact, he had informed those in charge that he wanted and was ready to get married, and he already knew me and my family. If it could be arranged with me as his wife, he would go back to his own hometown, so arrangements were made. All of this was unbeknownst to me! I would find out some time later in a prophetic, "God said." Please follow me for a moment. I knew the prophetic movement and according to the scriptures, when a prophet imposes a prophecy, it builds up, gives direction, uplifts, brings clarity and so on, but this just sent me into utter confusion.

I only knew *of* him, yes, very well, but ... we had never been out on an actual date! We only saw each other at church or when he visited our house with my brother. The only other things I knew about him was that he liked to eat a lot, he had small feet (about a size 8 ½ for a man of his size), who his people were, that he was the baby of the family and that he was honed in on me. I questioned my parents about this, and my mother said to me, "You have a relationship with God. He will direct you as to what you should do."

Days turned into weeks and weeks into a couple of months, still with no answer from God, until one night, I had a dream. I was getting married under a flowered tree and a Caucasian gentleman was marrying me as we were taking our vows. I said, "I do" and as I turned to say, "I do" to my groom, his face was shaded with no form. I woke up suddenly and Satan went to work on my thinking that this was a "go ahead" sign, which, in reality, it was NOT.

I Do

~~

On May 6, 1970, I was married and then reality set in. It was an entirely different world, and I said to myself, but not to God, "Please help me. What have I done?!" But it was done. I was married and there were no other thoughts of ever being able to leave; this was my life, so I was going to have to deal with it. I programmed myself into believing that I was happy when his or my relatives came around. I put my mind in another place to give them an enjoyable visit and not expose my real feelings. I acted like I was happy.

I experienced a state of life that I had never before known: utilities being shut off for non-payment, not having any food and having to "just stop by" at my sister's house. I stayed at her house just to see what she was cooking and eat more than one time. We did not have transportation of our own. I had to catch the bus ... when I had .50 cents. Ultimately, there were evictions. Lastly, the place where we met, he refused to return to. He had no desire to go back to church, but I continued to sing and praise God. It was all I had left, so I continued.

Many times, I went to church with an eviction notice in my pocketbook and many times saying to myself, "Do you really have to go back to the house with no lights and water?" But I did it only because I felt like I had no other choice. I would drown myself in the praises of God. It gave me strength to continue on.

Did Sister Shirley Nowell Carr get anything out of this marriage that was even remotely good? Yes, I did, by the names of Danetta Shirelle, Thomosa Daniele and Natasha Jeanine – my little ladies, and still are to this day, my ladies! Their father adored them to the point that he would occasionally say, "If you ever left me and took my girls, I'd hunt you down night and day until I found them." He didn't say this in a mean way, but in a serious manner.

One faithful night, December 28, 1978, at 9:15pm, there came a knock to the door; it was very unusual since we lived somewhat on the outskirts of town. Upon answering the door, it was my father, the prophet, delivering a message from God to my husband. With tears in his eyes, he pleaded for him to turn back to God, change his ways, and that this night was the night of salvation. The hand and call of God was upon him, and that tonight was the time of change. And then he turned and left the apartment, leaving us both in awe, for this was not the only time this same message had been given to him.

We started to go back to bed when a few minutes later, another knock came to the door. Had Daddy come back again? No, not again. It was the person my husband had been waiting for before my Daddy came. I just pretended to be asleep as I so often did in the past on the many nights between 12am and 6am, often hearing him getting out of a car and me being too afraid to see who he was getting out of the car with. No, I never asked, and he never said.

But on this particular night, I was shaken by him shortly after getting in. He was sick with pains in his chest. I thought he had been somewhere and had eaten something that was causing indigestion, but not so this time. It was the onset of a massive heart attack. I quickly went next door and called for help. Before finishing the phone call, I hear a loud bump. I ran back to the apartment and saw that he had fallen from the sofa onto his knees, and as I extended my hand to touch him, I felt a force pull my hand back. I knew then that it was God; we must learn when God is moving so that we can get out of His way. He never makes a mistake.

The ambulance came and proceeded to work on him, and in a few short minutes, he was in full cardiac arrest. They called his name several times, but received no answer. I knew then that maybe it was over; yes, that night, Earnest died 2 ½ hours after the prophet had warned him.

What goes through a person's mind when they are vulnerable? Only God knows. My husband was gone at age 26; he never had an opportunity to say goodbye to his children or me, his wife. From May 1970 to that night in December 1978, we'd moved 10 times due to evictions. We stayed often with my parents so that the girls had access to see their favorite TV show, "Sesame Street," as well as normal necessities that normal people, especially children, should have.

The next morning, the word got to his co-workers and his friends, and they all began to call and rush to visit me at my parent's home to find out what happened. And I repeated the story over and over again until I was utterly exhausted. My mother, knowing that I was tired having been up all night, asked if everyone would excuse us and leave. The word would get to them as to the arrangements, and they all did, except for one particular friend and that was a female who had sat on the floor at my knees. I thought maybe she had not heard my mother because she still sat there seemingly in utter shock. So, Ma repeated the request again and only then did she get up from off the floor and reluctantly proceeded to the door. But before she left, she requested to come back some time later to talk to me. Even though this seemed odd, and because I wanted her to leave, I said, "Of course!"

We found out later that she left mom and dad's house only to go to my sister's house two doors down, and even later, we found out that she was guilt-ridden and wanted to free herself. It was her house that my husband had been at that faithful night, and she also revealed what activities went on that night. She was the OTHER woman. Thank God for the very memory of my parents, John and Etta Nowell, who were there through all of this and never further degraded me by downgrading him, which could have been done and rightfully so, but they never did. From that very day to the present, I have never saw that woman again.

Single Parenting

~~

Starting the process of recuperating from the untimely death of Earnest, the three girl's father, I strongly felt I had to quickly get over my grief, pain and shock. I had to pull it together and make some plans for our future. The first challenge was to move out of my parent's home and secure a home of our own. Night and day, my thoughts were not of myself, but to try with everything in me to create a surrounding of security and stability for them. My conversation to myself was: *I am all they have left; they did not ask to be brought into this world nor this situation and they are my sole responsibility.*

Advice to single parents, women or men: being there for your children does not totally mean buying them everything they do or do not ask for. Yes, I was there for my daughters emotionally and all other ways that I was supposed to be, but 70% of it was buy, buy, buy. I did not realize that the prior situation I had lived in - lack and instability - was really over. Although mentally and emotionally it was still present, every time I had thoughts about what I was dealing with, I was prompted to take the girls out and buy them something. My thoughts were that I would make sure, with every fiber of my being, that my children would never live in poverty or live without the necessities of life the way I had after leaving my father's house. Going to church, supporting their school curriculums, outings to the park, recreational activities and quality time by ourselves was the norm for the girls and myself. And for that particular moment, it worked very well for the girls and me.

Another challenging aspect of single parenting is that each little girl had their own unique personality, and those personalities had to be approached in a strategic way. Being a one-parent entity, the responsibility is doubled and demands more attention than usual. Having three girls, there were times when I was pulled in three different directions and I learned to perfect it.

Daughter number one, the oldest, continuously talked without a breath in between; she needed to know that I was paying attention and listening to her. Whenever I needed to go to the kitchen, the bedroom, or bathroom, she was right behind me still talking continuously. There were times when in order for me to get a break, I would offer to give her a quarter to stop. Fascinated by the money, she would stop for a moment, but soon would go right back. Daughter number two was not so much a talker, but one of anger and sure mischief, which was evident in her actions: biting, scratching, and throwing things. Sitting in timeout, spanking, or being reprimanded, oftentimes, did not work with her. I had to strategically come up with ways to discipline her and still show her love. Eventually after many days of stern discipline, talks, and prayer, her anger and actions became more controllable, which made my life easier.

The last child to parent was daughter number three. She was the quiet one; unlike her sisters, she wasn't talkative or mischievous. She was a silent child that often cried under her breath, more or less a whimpering sound. It was hard to pull things out of her such as her feelings, emotions and words. Even with that obstacle, I was blessed to know exactly how to connect with her and pull the hidden things out. After some time, the quiet, sweet, silent child became more sociable and energetic, which helped when life changes began to happen.

I didn't realize it until later, but I had removed myself from my feelings, not making myself the priority, not dealing with my emotions, only because that's what I thought I was supposed to do so I could raise the girls. Also, in my thoughts, might I add, I thought that "this is not about me now, but them." Bu it did include me. I had not made peace with the unfortunate circumstances of my past and, in fact, I had brought the baggage right along with me. Buying, spending and more buying was truly an indication of it. I had to learn and completely make peace with my past; as a single parent, this is one of the best pieces of advice I offer. Also, allow yourself time to heal so that you can move forward with a clean slate and peace of mind.

Regardless of whatever situation that has brought you to the place of being a single parent, never being married, widowed, divorced, etc., understand and know God, Love, and a normally balanced life is a must have and need. This is not only for a child, (children), but adults as well, and after many years of overextending myself, I realized what I had to do: face the failures of the past, learn from them, and use them as a tool to create a brighter and blessed future. And do it without being bitter, but to be better.

What a relief it was to move on and be free of burdens! Although I'll always remember my past, my future was so much brighter, and the past will not have the same effect on me.

If there is a lesson to be learned from my experiences, that I have passed on to my children, who are now grown with their own families, that lesson is this: when you cleanse yourself of regrets and should've, could've, and would've, there's a positive giant waiting on you that is greater than your past; and when you realize it and release it, you learn I WILL NOT LIVE IN THE PAST.

Marry the One You Love

~~

Life goes on, as well as time, and that is what happened with the girls and me; time was the healer for us. The five year old, Danetta, being the oldest, she never asked where her father was; the four year old, Thomosa, I found out later on that she had seen her father on his knees going into cardiac arrest; and the two and half year old, Tasha, had conversations with him after the fact like he was not gone. We allowed her to do this until she eventually stopped.

A new house and new surroundings were in line for me and my daughters, and that is just what happened: a brand-new subdivision, never been occupied by anyone - just the thing. As the girls were playing outside one day, one of them came running inside to inform me that one of their dad's co-worker was coming towards the house. His name was Sylvester, aka, Sly. I came out to speak, and he gave his condolences and asked permission to a short visit with the girls; hesitantly, I gave permission and thanks to little prophetess, Thomosa, I learned that when their daddy would drop me off at church, on many previous occasions, they would ride with him and one of the occupants he picked up and hung out with: Mr. Sly. It was something else I did not know.

I allowed Mr. Sly to have the visit with the girls; I even invited him in for about 30 minutes. He asked if in the future he could come back for an occasional visit again and my reply was, "Maybe." But certainly not any time in the evening leading into night, and this was stressed several times simply because, as one would say, he had not been converted (saved) yet, and because of the morals I had been taught.

Shortly after Mr. Sly left, he called back to the house from a payphone to thank me and said that it meant a lot to him; he then told me to look under the lace tablecloth on the coffee table. He had left something for the girls; holding the phone, I proceeded to look and discovered he had left a hundred-dollar bill. I was mortified! I stressed to him that I would be returning it and he begged profusely for me to keep it for his friend's children. I cautiously kept it for a while until I felt his contribution was genuine.

From that moment on, my thoughts began to change about people, in general. The thoughts were that everybody had some good in them and that everyone was not just plain the Devil. This man had *good* in him and had no other motive except to contribute to our family.

Mr. Sly kept in contact occasionally by phone; he was genuinely concerned about us, but I felt I had to ask him to stop calling. He had no idea, but he showed me something that had not been previously shown to me: unselfishness and consistency, to name a few. It was so out of the norm for me that I thought it was devil-related, to somehow set me up, but in actuality, I was feeling a positive change in my heart towards him. I just didn't know it yet.

I made my mind up that if he ever called back, I would not be so distrusting and at least have a decent conversation with him. It took a minute, but he called back and asked to come over. I said yes, but, as we both stated at the same time, "Only in the daytime." Why not a nighttime visit? I didn't want him to come over at night. Not very much time had passed since my husband's death and to have a male visitor come during the evening into the night, to me, looked as well as seemed inappropriate, especially having girls. I didn't want to put myself or him in a compromising situation. I knew the Word of God and understood that the flesh was (and is) weak, and I did not want to take a chance on what could happen, but most of all, to have regrets. He was a perfect gentleman whenever he came over, but I was in careful mode.

This short visit changed my world: yes, concerning people. Everybody that is outside of the church "in the world," as we put it, does not want to be there. There is a reason they are still out there, and it is up to us that have "made it," so to speak up, to share how we overcame and to let them know that there is a better way; that way is JESUS!

Mr. Sly knew I went to church and that night, he asked me to pray for him. *Huh?!* I was stunned. He had heard about God through family members but had not accepted or followed through with their suggestions, and he wanted to know if I could help him find God. Good God Almighty! I said, "Yes I can," and from that moment, my assignment began. Assignment for what, you ask? To help him truly find out for himself who God truly was; from that day onward, he was no longer Mr. Sly, but Sylvester.

I alone knew what I had to do; others did not. Those that supposedly knew me thought I had lost my mind and left God for entertaining myself with a sinner; there were rumors along the way about me that I was doing things that I never had and/or would do to this day. There were too many people to try and explain and defend my actions to, so I let the rumors fly, and when I went to church, I got in the face of God and sang and PRAISED Him! Praising Him always gave me a release.

Mixed and Well-Blended

~~

Once I realized that Sylvester (Mr. Sly to the girls) had a very special place and a part of my heart, I felt without a doubt I wanted to marry him; the next thing was to address it to the girls, to help them transition from knowing and accepting him from Mr. Sly to stepdad. Unbelievably, it was no problem at all. This process was started before I became engaged to him; along with his visits in the "daytime," he saw my dedication to my children. I had stressed to him my intentions for their young lives. Without me telling him, he discerned each one of their personalities and would suggest ways to accommodate them and to give myself some me time.

Sylvester knew and shared with me that the oldest talkative child would one day use her talkative skills to make a living and needed books to occupy her over functioning mind. So, I kept her with books and it worked, even until this day. He also knew and helped me to realize that the second daughter's actions of fighting and misbehaving was perhaps seeing and knowing her father was gone, and as a child, not knowing how to express it, she felt angry and insecure. On one of his visits, she became sleepy, so he asked permission to take her in the room where her sisters were and lay her on the bed. I agreed and he did as he said he would. He told her to go to sleep and it worked; no more fighting her sisters, and no more biting or scratching or hiding. Miracles do happen.

For daughter number three, Ms. Quiety, she was his go to girl: 'get this for your Mom' and 'get this for your sisters' or 'do this for me.' Wow! Giving her some things to do got rid of the introvert in her.

The day soon came when Mr. Sly became a permanent fixture in our lives and a welcomed one was he; he went from Mr. Sly to "dad" by their own choice, even knowing who their biological father was. The title of "stepfather" or "stepdaughter," according to Sylvester, would never be used in our family because his explanation of the words indicated someone being stepped on and that would never happen. Trying to blend a family was just like blending and making a cake: first, you have the dry mix, then the eggs, the water and butter or oil, all very well mixed together. Then, and only then, can it be cooked and finished for consumption and perhaps shared with others.

In the Daytime (Marrying the Love of My Life)

~~

I fell in love with Sylvester, and on September 4, 1979, I married him. It did not matter whether anyone else was happy for me; it did not matter to me, and the girls were happy, happy, happy! My talks of God increased and his questions about God increased. Please learn these two vital lessons I am about to give you:

Lesson 1

When a person becomes an adult and whatever lifestyle they choose to live, even being a Christian, understand that they had to go through a process of time to get to where they are, and it is going to take a process of time to change. I knew this and did not expect Sylvester to do a complete U-turn immediately as long as he was getting it.

Lesson 2

Make sure you have made peace with your past and not drag it into the future of your new life. I learned this personally.

I was so relieved to have been free for Sylvester and myself to lovingly choose each other but being angry at the church world that got in the way of me giving him the fullness of the time for his complete transition. I was so happy that I overlooked the drinking problem he told me he was struggling with before I married him. And he struggled and we struggled. I might add that Sylvester fought with his monster; he never missed work, the bills were paid, we overate (he was a certified chef) and he was always apologetic and loving even when tipsy.

The times when he was most tipsy was when he really wanted to play the Shirley Caesar songs and get in the spirit, and he would call the girls to get in the spirit with him (r-i-g-h-t); and they would, too, by now with "Daddy." I would sit back and watch in awe; he'd cry and put his hands in the air, and cry out, "Yes, Lord!" tipsy. There were times, though, when I did not know whether it was alcohol or him, and I would tell him not to play with God. From a tear-stained face, he would try to explain this was greater than him and he just could not help it.

It wasn't until then that I realized what was happening and what I needed to do; his transition was taking place and I needed to gently push it. I put my hands in the air and asked

God to forgive me for holding onto anger, for moving out of timing and to wash over me again so that I could help this man.

OMG! My life turned around! If only God's people who are called by His name would humble themselves, seek His face and turn from their wicked ways, then will they hear from heaven and He will heal their land. My land was healed – so healed that we made a decision to leave Virginia and truly have a new start by moving back to North Carolina. For Sylvester, who had never been to North Carolina, this move was truly a new one, and a good one. We were leaving all bad experiences and memories behind for him and for me as well.

Several months before moving, my older sister had migrated back to North Carolina and had started a very blessed ministry; what God had invested in her was very much needed and proven for many at that time, and the timing for my family was perfect: leave one place and go into another with a new start and new, but yet, familiar ministry.

The girls were still young when we moved. And I, yet still excited, joined with my sister to do whatever was needed to help build the church: singing, ushering, being a part of the outreach ministry. The church grew. Sylvester, however, was still in the process of integrating into a different way of life for the better and had not joined the church yet, but he did promise to visit.

A revival had just been scheduled at the church. Without me asking, God sent Pastor Louise Branch, my sister and pastor at this time, to my house to invite Sylvester to come to the revival, and he agreed. Later that very night at the revival, God used the man of God who was conducting the revival, and who had never seen, nor knew my husband, to call him out and offer him a prayer. Hesitantly, my husband went up to the altar and, of course, I joined him. God completed the work on Sylvester Johnson that night, and, of course, as usual, I danced and praised God.

God truly saved this man and he lived it wherever we went; there were times in the process where he had mishaps, but he knew what to do: throw his hands in the air and call on God. He was my greatest supporter at the edge of the pulpit screaming for me to "Preach, Shirley!" after I was called to the ministry, or he'd join me on the church floor in the holy dance. I preached, praised, and glorified God, always remembering where He had brought us from.

To this union, we added two boys; yes, my two men: Dominic Sharod and Jareth O'Neal. I might add that I was 41 when I had Jareth against all medical odds between me and Sylvester, but God. He also blessed us to be able to do something neither one of us had ever done before; that was to buy not one, but two, houses side by side on the same street.

After faithful membership with Pastor Branch, in January 1988, God moved on me and opened a "God door." Victory Temple of Deliverance Church was opened in a small town called Boydton in Virginia. I had never heard of the town before, but it was a "God door" and He blessed us. Sylvester continued to stand at the edge of the pulpit, yelling, "Preachhhh, Shirley!" God proved himself in the membership and in the progress of the church. In my mind, thing could not get any better. The congregation was loving.

Sylvester made his mark in our lives and a good mark it was. He battled many complications of diabetes over the years, which also affected us all seeing him go through this battle. There were many days his feet and ankles would swell due to poor circulation. His eyesight was dwindling and, ultimately, he suffered from congestive heart failure.

It was Tuesday March 16, 1999: our regular day for bible study. As we prepared to go, Sylvester informed me that he was tired and was going to stay at home. I said ok and suggested that I should stay with him. I was going to send the children, but he insisted that he was fine; he was just tired and told me to go ahead and not miss service. So, I did go, but decided to leave the two boys with him (Dominic 18 years old and Jareth 6 years old). After being in bible study for about an hour and a half, I received a phone call from Dominic to come home right away because Dad had fallen out. He attempted to resuscitate him, but he did not respond, so he called 911 and the ambulance was on the way.

I immediately left bible class to see what was going on and as I approached my street, it was lined with a firetruck, police cars, and the ambulance. In my mind I was thinking, what had happened? Where was Jareth? As I approached my porch, my front door was wide open from so many officials that had responded to the call. And the first disturbing thing I saw was a very frightened 6-year-old boy at the foot of the bed, watching frantically as emergency personnel used a defibrillator to try a resuscitate his father on the floor in our room. In their haste to help Sylvester, they forgot to escort this young child from the scene.

I quickly removed Jareth from the room and rushed to Sylvester's side crawling under the EMT workers to get to him and hold his hand to reassure him that I was there. He had suffered a heart attack and was on his way out but not before squeezing my hand as a response to me that he knew I was there. After many unsuccessful tries, a final trip to the hospital, and the emergency room doctor putting in a pacemaker, it was over. The love of my life was gone, and his sons were the last to see him alive.

Second Peter 3:9 says, "The Lord is not slack concerning his promise as some men count slackness, but is longsuffering to us-ward, not willing that any should perish but that all should come to repentance." And most importantly of all, God knew their designated years on this earth: one at 26 and the other at 46. And that those men needed a chance at salvation, and the only way was through me. Shirley was the bait, and even through all the pain, it was ok with me.

Thank God for the never-ending support from the then members of the now one-year old Victory Temple Church. A one-year old ministry and a widow: there was nothing left to me but God who had brought me out before and kept my mind intact. That was the only way I had to go, in my mind, because when the "homegoing" service is over, everyone leaves, scatters, and goes back to their homes and their usual way of life, the recipient's way of life (mine) is forever changed. I needed and held onto God. Sylvester's "homegoing" was on Saturday and on the next day, Sunday, it was church as usual, and guess who preached? I did, and praised God. It was all I had left.

The house where Sylvester, my sons, Dominic and Jareth, my daughter, Tasha, and I harmoniously lived, soon became a place where Sylvester also took his last breath. It was unbearable for Jareth and Dominic to continue to stay there, so a decision was made to move to another house. Thank God both houses sold and Dominic, my son, moved out on his own and Tasha got married. Jareth struggled mentally and emotionally after seeing his father pass away until I was ordered by his school to secure counseling for him; we did this for two years.

Truthfully, it helped. I saw that if Jareth was in the same town of the tragedy, he could not, as a young child, move on and, thus, we decided to move back to Virginia. This time, it wasn't to Charlottesville where I was years before, but to a little town called South Hill. Yes, move, move, move! But don't forget that I was used to it.

I prepared to find and purchase a house in the small town of South Hill, Virginia. By this time, Tasha was already living there. I loved it; it was small, and this was another new beginning. I soon found the house I wanted and prepared to purchase it; a closing date was set with the closing cost of $1,500.00. "I got this," is what I said to myself, and I did. I was preparing to move out of the sold house, but at the last minute, the closing was changed, and then changed again; this went on for three months. Jareth, who was just coming out of pain, was thrown back in it. We had no house of our own; yes, we stayed with his older siblings and was more than welcomed to never leave – going from North Carolina to Virginia. We also stayed in hotels. But young Jareth was used to his own room in our own house and not living out of the backseat of our car.

One day, tearfully, he told to me that he wanted to go home and asked why we couldn't go home. I explained to him that we had sold the house and we were going to move, and he said, "Why would you sell one house and didn't have another one to live in?" I was so choked up, I couldn't answer right away. So, I took him to his favorite place, Walmart, to buy him a toy, and the distraction worked!

Finally, after seven closing dates and nine financial institutions to finance the loan, we were ready to go, but not before they informed me that the bank that had financed my closing and the cost had gone from $1,500.00 to $20,000. You have got to be kidding me!! I did not have $20,000, but my God did. I scheduled a revival in the midst of all of this mess and it was the right thing to do. I did not reach out to the church for help. I truly did not know where to even seek this amount of money. I simply prayed.

The woman of God came in under the power of the Holy Ghost; her name was Pastor Carolyn Faines, and the first thing she did was to brandish a pair of shoes with a hound's tooth pattern. It was black at the tip and she declared that God said someone was going to be there – someone that needed a breakthrough – and that believing and receiving them would bring victory. It would destroy the plans of the enemy, and when she finished, she further stated that the shoes were a size nine. I expected at least four or five women to run up to receive them, but no one came forth.

I stood to help further push what God had said through this woman-servant and before I could speak, the Lord spoke to me and said, "It's you. The shoes are for you, and wherever the soles of those shoes tread, the land will be given to you." I understood my breakthrough was not in the hound's tooth shoes, but in the faith of what God had said. I quickly took off my shoes and put on the shoes brought by the woman of God and they fit like a glove.

Needless to say, I danced a while in the victory shoes, and when service was over, I instructed my children to take me to the house where I would be living, and they did. Upon arriving at 11pm that night, I ran across the yard with the "For Sale" sign still in the yard and put the shoes inside the screen door and left with no doubt that it was done! And it *was* done.

Give Me My Keys!

~~

The homelessness was over and done with; the insecurity for the sad little boy who wanted to go home was gone. No more switching closing dates, no more denial from more banks and last, but not least, the $20,000 was covered. God had touched a woman of God who wrote me a check for $5,000 and my older brother, Bishop William Nowell, gave me a signed blank check and told me to fill it in with what I needed. And when all of this was finished, I had what I needed. God bless unselfish people who are not afraid to show into others without fear. God keeps His promises; if He said it, He is able to perform it.

Not many days hence closing on my home, while in the attorney's office signing papers, I discerned the enemy thinking he still had won and perhaps I did not have the amount needed to close. I was asked two times about the asked for amount and two times I answered, "Where do I sign?"

Once all the paperwork was finished, they said, "We are done. Twenty thousand dollars, please."

And I proudly slid the certified check across the table and said in a loud voice, "Give me my keys!"

I got my keys and the mountain of paperwork and rushed three hours away to Henderson, NC to a crowd of baptized believers waiting for me to bring a praise report and expound on the Word of God; and God met us there. I gladly screamed, "Jesus Never Fails!" The power of God fell, and I did not forget to praise God in a dance. Everyone in the building joined me in praising and worshiping God after hearing my testimony. Not just because of my words, but by the sincerity felt through my praise. I was able to preach from a place that I had never preached before. This place was a place of restoration and freedom from the despair that I felt for many years and dealt with privately.

August 2005 was the beginning of the end of evictions and being homeless. Now, I only stay at hotels at my leisure. The Devil thought he had me, but I got away and I moved into my miracle home a place that I prayed for: my miracle home a place where tall, white columns stood in support for the front porch, which was a symbol to me that this home would support and offer the security that Jareth and I so needed. The spacious dining room were many prayers of thanks and countless Sunday dinners with my children and grandchildren would take place, the serene screened in back porch served as the perfect after dinner relaxation spot. Our home not only provided the space we needed, but this home served as a reminder to me that no matter what struggles life may bring, if you have faith and believe, all things are possible.

I share my stories to encourage others that there is hope and that hope is in Christ Jesus. Jareth had his own room again where he felt safe and not afraid to sleep in a neighborhood with lots of friends and a new school. The church was prospering and growing. Deacon Sylvester was sorely missed by all, but we had consolation that surely if offered an opportunity to come back, perhaps he would not, and it was ok. I was greatly at peace knowing that Sylvester was now resting and all of things that we planned for our future were beginning to happen.

The Test of My Faith

~~

Victory Temple grew and we began fellowshipping with other ministries in Virginia, North Carolina and New Jersey; it was a blessing. One faithful Sunday, I arrived at church only to notice my daughter, Thomosa, waiting outside pacing in front of the church. I got out of the car and asked her if something was wrong. She quickly responded that there was a young man inside and "he says he's our brother and wants to see you." My response was that it was a joke and I was going to fix it.

I walked into the church and spotted the only stranger in the building with a young lady and five boys. I motioned to the devotional leader to continue the service and invited the young man into my study. My thoughts were that this was some kind of joke, and he was playing it on me at my church. I proceeded to introduce myself and he said, "I know." I asked who he was and he said very humbly, "I am Earnest Carr, Jr., and I just came to formerly meet you and my sisters."

How could this be? By now, Earnest Sr. had been deceased for years and I had never even heard of an Earnest Jr. I started with the questioning as to how old he was and he answered, to my surprise, that he was two years older than our oldest daughter, Danetta. I then asked where he had been all these years, and that we knew nothing about him. And he answered, "They knew," meaning his father's people, especially his father, who just *supposedly* kept him a secret from us.

The next question to him was proof of who he was saying he was. "Do you have proof that you are who you say you are?" I inquired further.

He then went into his wallet and pulled out a very old, tattered, folded birth certificate, which stated that Earnest Sr. was indeed the father as well as a very old and folded obituary of his dad. That was all he had. My next question was, "Did your father ever have any visits or interactions with you as a child?" His answer was no, but that his brothers did.

What a stunning as well as shocking situation to have to deal with on a Sunday morning! My daughters had a brother that knew about then, but we knew nothing about him. What was I to do? Get angry? Call somebody and tell them off? But who? And then the Holy Ghost kicked in and began speaking to me and said, "You are both not victims, but survivors, so introduce him to your dolls and the congregation." I brought him up and introduced him as my girls' brother; no one looked confused, but simply joined in and we had church.

Thank God for the pillars of strength I had with me then: Mother Mabel McKnight, Minister Celestine Jefferson, Evangelist Pattie Williams and the one and only Prophetess Sula Steed. Years later, they, too, met Sylvester and went on to be with the Lord. That day and until now, Earnest Jr. is not just my girls' brother, but my son, and a blessing it is. I still had to preach that day and did so.

The following five years proved to also be one of the most testing times of my life; it seemed that after all I had survived and that I was now in a good place in my life, my health started to take a nose-dive. Year after year, one thing after another hit me, yet I managed to still trust in God because He was all I had. There were times when an all-nighter would be called at church; through prayer and consecration, the saints not knowing my plea to God, and as faithful as He is, He would always come through. But I had to keep myself together in the meantime.

July 2008

After coming home one day from church, I felt a constant pain in my stomach that would not go away. I thought that after resting and taking some over-the-counter medication, it would go away, but it did not. So, I decided to go to the emergency room to have it checked out, thinking it was something minor. After being there for hours, the results were in; I had a condition I had never heard of before: diverticulosis, a condition that involves the intestines, wherein, they develop small sacs on the digestive tracks. Grainy food items get trapped in them and, thus, do not move out of the intestines as they should; they become bacteria and could become deadly if not treated in time. Thank God mine was caught in time; recovery varies, but for me, it took seven days. I was released just in time to go home, get dressed and go to church that very same day. Praise God! The congregation never even knew. Praising Him was all I had left, and it pushed me to continue.

July 2009

Another year passed and I knew what to do to avoid episodes of the intestine problem, but despite doing the right things, I had another episode the exact same time as the year before. This was unreal! My doctors agreed but admitted me anyway and went to work to get me better. Another seven days and victory later, but why the same time from last year?

July 2010

I was blessed to be invited to go out of the country on mission trips with the ministry of Pastor Lisa Veney. She had taken the gospel to many who needed what other converts had to offer about the true and living God. Before I left to join her, I had another episode of diverticulitis and this one was worse than the times before, and yes, I ended up back in the hospital the very same time as before. The doctors agreed that this episode was, in fact, worse and went to work on me, but this time, they warned me that if the episodes continued, surgery would be imminent. I informed my doctor of my plans to go out of the country and he was sorely against it knowing that many foreign countries have illnesses and fevers that could be contracted, especially in my vulnerable state. I prayed to God concerning my desire to take my praise and testimony to others; I wanted to go.

Unexpectedly, my doctor called me back and asked me where it was abroad that I wanted to go, and I told him. And out of his mouth he said, "I release you to go, but look into getting a yellow fever shot." It wasn't mandatory but it was good to have it, and then he told me where to go and get one. As he finished with his instructions on the shot, I thanked him and informed him that this last episode with diverticulitis would be my last because I was healed. Needless to say, he was at a loss for words, and responded, "Alright, Mrs. Johnson. Take care and look into getting the shot."

Did I go out of the country? Yes, and in a mighty way to Suriname, South America. Did I get the shot? I won't answer that. Did I end up in the hospital in July 2011 with another episode? No! I have not had another episode to this day! My God is a healer and you have what you say - proclaim - to have. I proclaimed "healing."

May 2011

I was diagnosed with gallstones; an x-ray had revealed numerous stones, thus, a decision was made to remove the gallbladder. Praise God for that decision. They discovered during the surgery that the amount of gallstones that I had were on the brink of causing a toxic infection and complete dysfunction of my gallbladder. But God!

July 2012

What I thought was just another digestive upset, x-rays revealed that my appendix was about to rupture and was swollen three times its normal size. Emergency surgery was performed by Dr. Tozzi; he later told my children that the removal occurred just in time because my appendix had gangrene, which was, ironically, only confined to one area of the appendix. It normally spreads all over the organ. But God!

August 2013

After so many surgeries, it was the norm for my doctors to have me come back once a year for any concerns I might have and to do a routine check-up. At one particular visit, I voiced my concerns again about discomfort I was having on my right side, acid reflux, perhaps, from past experiences.

Oh well! Not this time! As usual, an x-ray was scheduled and, once again, something showed up that neither I nor my doctor liked. It was a quarter-sized spot on my pancreas, and it was unexplainable as to how or when it got there. He could not suggest exactly what it was, so he sent me to one of his colleagues at a bigger and more experienced hospital. I knew that he was not going to say what he thought it might be, but I trusted God.

My children were in the dark or acted as such as to why I had to go to another town for testing. They said not a word but took me to the appointment. After arriving at the hospital, I was instructed to go sign in, but then they realized what was going on: yes, they were testing and getting ready to do a biopsy on what they thought was pancreatic cancer. I was put under and the test began.

After being awakened by the nurses, one of them informed me that they had a time with me even being under anesthesia. I asked them what they meant, and they said, "You had three instruments down your throat, and you kept trying to talk, and by the way, do you know a foreign language?"

I was confused, so I said no, and they said that it surely sounded like it. And suddenly, in the wheelchair while being taken back to my room to join my family, the foreign language started again. Needless to say, it was the tongues of the Holy Ghost making intercession while I was under.

I joined my family in the waiting room and learned that the doctor had visited with them and had informed them that what had been seen on the previous x-ray was nowhere to be found, and an extra test was done only to reveal nothing! The doctor also informed my daughters that his fee for the procedure was over $10,000, but that the cost was on him and I was free to go. I praised Him all the way home for the miracle-working power of God.

My New Normal

~~

Rev. Clay Evans once wrote the following words to a song:

> When I look back over my life
> And I think things over
> I can truly say that I've been blessed
> I got a testimony.

My testimony has spilled over into a story, my true story, and as I was going through life, I often thought, "Why me?" or if there was something wrong with me. God allowed me to question myself over the years until one day, He revealed the answers to my questions, and the answers were the same words He gave to Jeremiah: "Before I formed thee in the belly, I knew thee; and before thou camest forth out of the womb, I sanctified thee, and I ordained thee a prophet unto the nations" (Jeremiah 1:5).

In other words, my life before my mother knew it, before my father knew it, and certainly before I knew it, was ordained by God and the things that Satan thought would hinder the plans of God for my life, God turned around for my good.

There are things I had dreamed of doing, but situations and circumstances at the time made it seem impossible and certainly not ever to become reality – traveling, for one. And now it has become an exciting norm. I've been blessed to have been to several cities in South America: Suriname, French Guiana, Paramaribo, and Mongos, to name a few. I have been blessed to have visited the Caribbean, Aruba, Curacao, Trinidad, the Bahamas, the Florida Keys, Cozumel (Mexico) and Europe (London, United Kingdom), Amsterdam, Belgium, Holland, and my journey continues.

The feeling of being able to have a choice is freedom all by itself; a choice as to which way you want to wear your hair, being able to go shopping and have enough money to get what you want and not have to beg for it; a choice that you can wear a skirt when you want to and a pair of pants when you are gardening without fear of breaking a Church Governed Rule. Rules that promoted the fear of God striking you down or the "Older Saints" reprimanding you for breaking a rule in which I interpreted to mean that God was more concerned about what you wore and not where your heart was concerning him. I now have the choice not to cook a full course meal every day; I can eat a salad and crackers if I choose to. Hallelujah! Who the Son set free is free, indeed!

My new normal is that every day, God truly reveals himself to me as to who He really was and is now: one who does not change and does not count slack as man counts slackness. He is in all and through all. I now see God as one that will never put more on you than you can bear. Merciful and understanding is His name; He is God of love and peace. Control and fear have never been nor ever will be the nature of our God.

I no longer live in fear as to what man can do to me. No longer do I live in a natural or spiritual STRAIGHT JACKET. Who the Son set free is free, indeed! I am holy because He is holy. I see men and women as *men* and *women*, and not as trees. Simply meaning, I see people the way they were intended to look, and in a clear and correct way. We are all God's creation, and learning Him for myself has brought freedom to my life and a never-ending praise to Him from me.

The Queen of Praise

~~

I, Apostle Shirley Johnson, do hereby formerly accept the title of "Queen of Praise." This title was given to me by my social media followers who, on a weekly basis, have watched me praise God in a dance and a push others to do the same. For this reason, I understand and know assuredly that had it not been for the Lord God Almighty by my side, I would not even be alive to share the story of my survival, my deliverance, my healings and my breakthroughs. Leaving my father's house allowed me to experience a different world and fight for my survival. I truly understand that it is not by power, not by might, but by His spirit and loving kindness shown towards me that I made it.

People, places, and things are memory makers in an individual's life and in my life, the three played major role, but the greatest memory-maker of all for me was, of course, my parents whom I have talked about throughout my story. My father continues to be that strong pillar for me even until this day even though he is no longer physically with us. He passed away of prostate cancer on December 28 in 1994. I remember the days of being at his bedside seeing him very weak and him still trying to get up and to fight it; to the bitter end, from his bedside, he was instructing and encouraging his children and grandchildren of the things that they should remember and do.

My mother was never the same after his death; she would often sit and stare into space, and when asked what she was thinking about, she would answer that John had left her. We knew perhaps it was just a matter of time for her, so each sibling took turns caring for her until it was impossible. On December 10, 1995, 18 days shy of a year, my mother passed on to be with my dad, John. Gone, but can never be forgotten, and they will always be in our hearts.

These two people shaped my life and molded me into the person I am today. Leaving my home as a young adult, I realized I stepped into what seemed to be another dimension. Thank God that my faith in God and determination not to give up has been the determining factor that I am still here to declare that my worst is over and my best is yet to come!

The ultimate question stands: "What shall I render unto God for all His blessings?" What shall I give? I have decided that for the rest of my life, I will give a loud "thank you" and a never-ending praise. Yes, I am also called to preach the gospel, but I also must take the time and commune with God. I am also still active in outreach to others, but PRAISE is what I do and is my way of expressing my admiration to Him, my way to applaud Him, the way I celebrate and love Him. God is the very source of my existence and my assignment here on earth. Hallelujah!!

If you want to learn how to praise Him, too, then here are a few ways you can begin:

Here are some great ways to express yourself in Praise

1. Lift your hands (Psalm 134:2): Lift up your hands in the Sanctuary and bless the Lord.

2. Praise Him with words (Hebrews13:15): Therefore by Him let us continually offer sacrifice of praise unto God, that is the fruit of our lips, giving thanks to His name.

3. Praising God with dancing and instruments (Psalm 149:3): Let them praise His name with the dance; let them sing praises to him with the timbrel and harp.

4. Do whatever you need to do to express your thanks to God.

When I Left My Daddy's House
By Shirley Johnson

Shirley Johnson

Apostle Shirley Ann Johnson was born Shirley Ann Nowell to Deacon John W. Nowell and Mother Mary E. Nowell, in Henderson, NC, on October 6, 1951. From that Date until she received Christ, it was known and told to her by her parents that a special call was on her life.

At the early age of nine, her family moved to Charlottesville, VA where they supported and was blessed through various ministries. She attended Charlottesville Public schools where she graduated from Lane High School, and then furthered her education at Jefferson Professional Institute, earning her public school teaching certification.

Apostle Johnson met and married Deacon Sylvester Johnson. God blessed them with their children: Danetta, Thomosa, Natasha, Dominic and Jareth. Through the years, God has added more children to her life (in laws): Semaj Mcknight, Anthony Dixon, Derrick Crayton, and Stephanie Wiggins. She also is the grandmother of five (5): Jalen, Semaja', Henre', Josiah, and Jaden.

In the early eighties, she moved back to Henderson, NC to work in ministry with her sister, Overseer Louise Branch. Being faithful in the ministry, she oversaw most of the ministry auxiliaries. Remaining hardworking and putting God first, she heeded the call of an evangelist. In April of 1984, Apostle Johnson became a licensed Evangelist, and in later years, became co-pastor of Crusade Pentecostal Deliverance Church where she served for twelve years.

Apostle Johnson not only expanded spiritually but also naturally. In May of 1993, she attended the North Carolina Justice Academy in Salemburg, NC, and became a full time corrections officer. She also successfully completed a number of academic courses at Vance Granville Community College. She became a licensed Notary Public, a substitute teacher, and eventually a Sergeant and the local jail facility, where she retired in the year 1999.

God saw that she was a diligent servant and told her to go into the Hedges and Highways, and compel men and women to come to him. In January of 1998, she stepped out on faith and was consecrated as the pastor of Victory Temple of Deliverance Church in Boydton, VA. As the ministry grew in leaps and bounds, God once again called her higher and added under her wings Jireh Deliverance Ministries, in Henderson, NC. In January 2013, God once again elevated Apostle Johnson as she was consecrated and deemed Chief Apostle of Kingdom Builder's International Fellowship of Church, which consisted of several of ministries.

Continuing to spread the gospel, God opened international grounds to Apostle, and she was able to share the word in various places such as Suriname, South America, Aruba, Paramaribu, French Guyana, Curacao, and Amsterdam, Holland, any other countries.

Apostle Johnson is a woman that exemplifies God's favor, His grace, and His humility in every aspect of her life. Through many trials and tribulations, she can say that she's still here and daily lives by Psalms 34:1: I WILL BLESS THE LORD AT ALL TIMES. HIS PRAISE SHALL CONTINUALLY BE IN MY MOUTH.

SOCIAL MEDIA

Follow Apostle Johnson on:

Facebook – Apostle Shirley Johnson

Instagram - @apostlejohnson_

Visit her website

@

www.apostleshirleyjohnson.com

CPSIA information can be obtained
at www.ICGtesting.com
Printed in the USA
LVHW010137291019
635545LV00009B/3811